[redacted]

THE CREATION OF THE

DANNY FINGEROTH

The Rosen Publishing Group, Inc.,
New York

For my mom, who shows me every day what real strength is
and who knows full well that "people are stranger than anybody"

Published in 2007 by The Rosen Publishing Group, Inc.
29 East 21st Street, New York, NY 10010

First Edition

Thanks to Marvel Entertainment, Inc.: Avi Arad, James Hinton, Mary Law, Bruno Maglione, Tim Rothwell, Mickey Stern, Alberta Stewart, and Carl Suecoff

Library of Congress Cataloging-in-Publication Data

Fingeroth, Danny.
The creation of the X-Men/Danny Fingeroth.—1st ed.
    p. cm.—(Action Heroes)
Includes bibliographical references and index.
ISBN 1-4042-0762-7 (lib. bdg.)
1. X-Men (Fictitious characters) I. Title. II. Series.
PN6728.X2F54 2006
741.5'973—dc22

2005037507

Manufactured in the United States of America

On the cover: The team featured in the *Astonishing X-Men* comic (*from left*, Wolverine, Emma Frost, Cyclops, Kitty Pryde, and the Beast), races into action in this illustration by John Cassaday.

CONTENTS

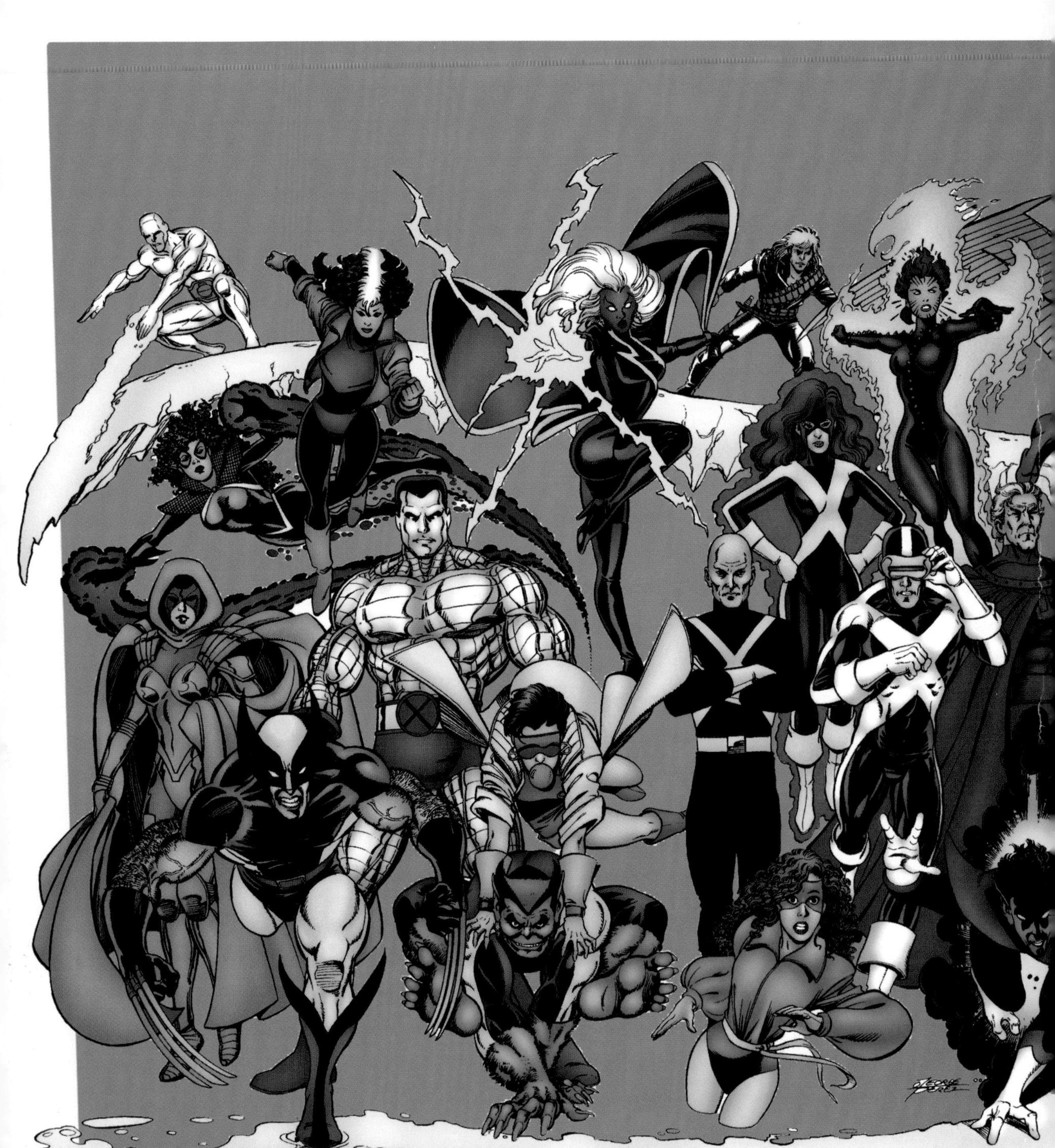

INTRODUCTION

The early 1960s was a great time for fans of action hero comics. Marvel Comics had had great success with *The Fantastic Four* and *The Amazing Spider-Man*. The new approach that had been taken by editor in chief and head writer Stan Lee was proving extremely popular. Comic readers had never seen characters like the Marvel heroes and villains. They had never read stories like the Marvel stories.

The big difference in what Marvel was doing came down to a few key elements. Most action hero comic stories until then were focused on plot. And most plots were pretty standard stuff. Aside from their powers, the heroes were all very similar. They were dedicated to upholding the law and went about it in a direct way, chasing and capturing criminals and handing them over to the police. Any humor they brought to their jobs was simplistic and obvious. (For instance, upon capturing a villain whose power was creating cold, a hero might brag that he or she had "put him on ice.") They never bickered in a serious way. Even if, like Batman, their origins were based on terrible childhood events, the heroes were never mean, moody, or petty.

The villains had more variety in aim but not in personality. They wanted money or power, or possibly just to cause trouble for the sake of causing trouble. They laughed with glee when they trapped the heroes. The idea that a villain might have some deep reason for being a villain was considered too complicated for what was seen as a medium for little kids.

With *The Fantastic Four*, which Lee co-created in 1961 with artist Jack Kirby, Marvel had shown that a story could deal with the interactions of characters with clashing personalities. The team's Thing character was a monster who hated the way he looked, despite the fact that his superstrength made him able to fight Super Villains like Dr. Doom.

Doom himself was the tyrant of a small country and thought he was the fairest ruler. He wanted to extend that blessing to the rest of the world. As far as Doom was concerned, he was the hero, and the Fantastic Four were the villains! As Lee said in an interview with Web site yesterdayland.com, "I like things to not always be black and white. I like the villain to be interesting in his or her motive."

Marvel's Spider-Man was a teenage hero, which was unheard of at the time. Before Spider-Man, teens were only sidekicks to adult heroes, like Robin was to Batman. "Spidey" was also a hero who was often unsure he was doing the right thing. He had money troubles. The public often thought he was a menace. All these complexities were brand-new for Super Heroes.

Marvel's gambles paid off. Audiences of the time were ready for something new, and they had found it in the Marvel approach. Lee then wanted to expand on Marvel's success with something new. Atomic radiation and its effects were on people's minds. Popular science fiction books and movies of the 1950s and 1960s often dealt with fears of what radiation could do to a person.

One of the feared effects was mutation. A mutation is a permanent change in a person or animal or even a plant. The mutation can be passed on to offspring and become the norm for an entire species. This usually occurs over long periods of time. But there was concern that atomic radiation could speed up the process.

In the years since the first atomic bombs were detonated in the 1940s, there had been much testing of atomic weapons by the United States and Russia. People were concerned about what the effects of the radiation produced by the nuclear blasts might be. Could it mutate humans? Would we all become freaks?

Lee called once again on artist Jack Kirby to co-create a new comic series based on these concerns. They came up with the idea that radiation could cause mutations that would give people super-powers. They added the twist that such people would need training in how to use those powers. They then added the concept that, while some mutants would want to use their powers for good, others would use them for evil, selfish purposes. Lee and Kirby then supposed that non-mutants would be afraid of mutants. If mutants were a warning that all humanity could be changing, that was scary enough. But what if some superpowered mutants wanted to take over the world?

Lee called the good mutants "the X-Men." As he and Kirby established it, the X-Men's role was to fight those evil mutants. But because the world was scared of all mutants, the world hated the good and evil ones alike. The original X-Men team consisted of the Angel, the Beast, Marvel Girl, Iceman, and Cyclops. They were led by Professor Charles Xavier (Professor X) and based out of Xavier's School for Gifted Youngsters.

The X-Men combined the bickering elements of *The Fantastic Four* with the troubled-teenager elements of *Spider-Man*. To that, Lee and Kirby added the twist that mutants were part of a persecuted minority group. At a time in the United States when the civil rights movement was on everyone's mind, *The X-Men* seemed bound to be an instant sensation.

Actually, the series often struggled in sales. New X-Men stories ceased to be created after 1970. Five years later, the series was relaunched and became the media juggernaut it is today. But we're getting ahead of ourselves. All your questions about the X-Men will be answered in the pages that follow—including *why* they're called the X-Men!

1 THE MEN BEHIND THE X-MEN

Stan Lee was born Stanley Martin Lieber in New York City on December 28, 1922. He lived in the Washington Heights section of Manhattan. Although a short subway ride from the glitz and glamour of Times Square, the Heights was a quiet neighborhood of middle-class and working-class families. Stan's father was often unemployed. This taught him that he never wanted to be without enough money to survive.

Young Stan loved to read. He read a wide range of short stories and novels, including many by Mark Twain and William Shakespeare. He also read modern tales of the adventures of characters such as Tom Swift, Tarzan, and Poppy Ott. Stan loved the newspaper comic strips of the time, too, including *The Katzenjammer Kids*.

In this era before television and the Internet, if Stan wasn't reading, he was likely to be found at the movies watching

Writer Stan Lee, co-creator of the X-Men, attends the premiere of the second X-Men movie in 2003. Lee is also the co-creator of Spider-Man, the Fantastic Four, and many other world-famous characters.

the exciting characters played by actors like Errol Flynn. The movie theaters also showed serials. Serials were short movies that were presented in weekly chapters. Like a comic book or a TV show today might have an ending that makes you want to read or see the next part, movie serials created antici-pation and suspense with cliffhangers.

Stan also grew up when radio drama and variety shows were popular. Families would gather around the radio to hear their favorite programs. Some of Stan's favorites were the adventure series *Chandu the Magician* and the comedy *The Jack Benny Show.*

At one point, Stan thought that he would become an actor. He worked for a time in the 1930s for the famous Works Progress Administration (WPA) Theater Project, which gave him stage train-ing. (The WPA was a federal program created to provide jobs for unemployed people—including those who worked in the arts— during the Great Depression.) After graduating from high school, Stan needed to find a job. His mother's cousin was married to a man named Martin Goodman, who owned a company that published comic books. Though he and Goodman didn't know each other well, Goodman hired Stan as an assistant at Timely Comics, the company that would eventually become Marvel.

HERE COMES KIRBY

Jack Kirby was born Jacob Kurtzberg on August 28, 1917. He grew up on the Lower East Side of Manhattan. The high-rises and limousines of the wealthy areas of the island might as well have been a million miles away from Kirby's slum neighborhood.

Kirby taught himself to draw and write and set out to make a living using those skills. One of the first places Kirby worked was the Fleischer Brothers' animation studios in Queens, across the river from Manhattan. There, Kirby drew cartoons starring Popeye the Sailor.

After working at the animation studio, Kirby started writing and drawing newspaper comic strips and editorial cartoons for magazines. This led him to the world of comic books, which needed talented artists. There, he had the opportunity to work with the legendary Will Eisner, who many people consider the inventor of the modern-day graphic novel.

Kirby then went to work for Fox Comics, where he met another young writer-artist, Joe Simon. Simon and Kirby hit it off. They would continue to work together whenever possible. In 1939, while still working for Fox, Simon became the first editor of Timely Comics. (At the time, working for competing companies was not considered unusual.)

In this photo from the 1950s, Jack Kirby poses with his wife, Roz, and children, Neal and Susan. Kirby was the primary artist who gave the Marvel comic line its distinctive look and feel. He also co-created the Fantastic Four, Captain America, and the Hulk.

A SUPER TEAM

In 1940, Kirby was hired as staff artist at Timely. Besides doing their own work, he and Simon were in charge of the writers and artists who produced the company's comics. Simon and Kirby were a successful and popular team. They shared writing and drawing duties, since each could do both. Together they co-created Captain America, a hit action hero for Timely.

Later that year, when their workload became too great, Martin Goodman provided them with an assistant: Stanley Martin Lieber. Working for Simon and Kirby, Lieber jumped at a chance to have his first story published. It was a two-page story (told in words, with only a couple of small illustrations) that appeared in 1941's *Captain America Comics* #3. Wanting to save his real name for the great novels he was sure he would someday write, Lieber signed the story with the name "Stan Lee," created by breaking his first name into two.

At the end of 1941, Simon and Kirby left Timely after disagreements with Goodman. Goodman made Lee editor until he could find a permanent replacement. He never did need to find one. Lee would remain editor (and, as the company grew, editor in chief) of Timely and then Marvel until he was promoted to publisher in 1972.

Comic books were very popular from the late 1930s until the late 1940s. By the 1950s, they began to go through periods of higher and lower sales. One cause for the dip in sales was the public outcry some teachers and politicians made over negative effects comics might be having on children. Also, the then-new medium of television stole readers' time and attention from comics.

During this period, Lee wrote and edited countless comic stories of all types for Timely, which had by then become known as Atlas Comics. But by 1961, he was getting tired of comics. He was preparing to quit when his wife suggested that before he go he try

THE 1960S: A TIME OF CHANGE

The 1960s (and the early part of the 1970s) was an era of unprecedented change. While the 1950s are often looked back upon as dull, the 1960s were full of drama. The assassination of President John F. Kennedy, the war in Vietnam, the civil rights movement, and the development of a "youth culture" by many of the 75 million baby boomers, all contributed to a sense of change.

In that climate of possibility, Marvel came out with comic books like no one had ever seen. *The Fantastic Four*, *The Amazing Spider-Man*, and *The X-Men* injected new life into the Super Hero genre.

doing comics in a way he would find interesting. *Justice League of America,* a comic about a team of Super Heroes, was having great success for DC Comics. Goodman told Lee that Atlas needed a Super Hero team, too.

Also around this time, Kirby had come back to Atlas. He and Simon had ended their partnership. Since his return in 1958, he and Lee had been co-creating short monster stories. Lee's response to his wife's suggestion was to co-create, with Kirby, *The Fantastic Four.* The series was a huge success, and Marvel (as the company was by then called) followed it with other characters, including Thor and the Hulk. Another big Marvel success was *The Amazing Spider-Man*, co-created by Lee and artist Steve Ditko.

Lee and his creative partners were telling stories that, while still set in a fantastic world, were more realistic than superhero comics had ever been. Now, Marvel wanted to come up with the next step in this new style of Super Heroes. That next step would be *The X-Men.*

2 SCHOOL'S IN SESSION

The X-Men was very much a product of its time. The 1960s was a period of great change in the United States and around the world. The baby boom generation (those born between 1946 and 1964) was the largest in American history. The issues important to them were reflected in much of the fiction they consumed, as well as in the music they enjoyed.

James Bond and other superspies, such as the ones from television's *The Man From U.N.C.L.E.*, were very popular when the X-Men were created. *The Lord of the Flies* was a popular novel and movie about kids building their own society—for better and for worse. In music, the Beatles and Bob Dylan were taking teenage pop music to another level of poetry and popularity.

In the comic world, the new Marvel characters were very popular. At rival DC Comics, the top sellers were *Superman*, *Batman*, and *Justice League of America*. It was into this world that the X-Men were born.

A NEW APPROACH

Lee and Kirby were looking for a new angle from which to approach superheroes. They combined several ideas. The first was the idea of a common origin for groups of superheroes and supervillains. The common origin was mutation, a change in a characteristic of a member of a species.

Mutation occurs in nature at a specific moment in time to a single individual. If the mutation is beneficial to a species, the new characteristic can, over a long period of time, become the norm for that species. It has been shown that radiation could cause mutations to occur with greater frequency. This was touched upon in such science fiction novels as 1953's *Children of the Atom* by Wilmar Shiras. In the movies, Godzilla was the product of mutation.

Lee and Kirby decided that their mutants would be hated and feared by the rest of society, who would fear that "normal" humans would be replaced by mutants. The public would see good and evil mutants as all the same. As Lee said in an interview with the Web site yesterdayland.com, "The evil mutants felt they should rule the world because they were the next stage in evolution above *homo sapiens*, just the way Cro-Magnon man was the next step in evolution over Neanderthal Man."

The cover of *The X-Men* #1 (*right*), drawn by Jack Kirby and Paul Reinman, is one of the most famous covers in the history of comics. It was the world's first glimpse of the Angel, the Beast, Marvel Girl, Cyclops, and Iceman, as well as their most important enemy, Magneto.

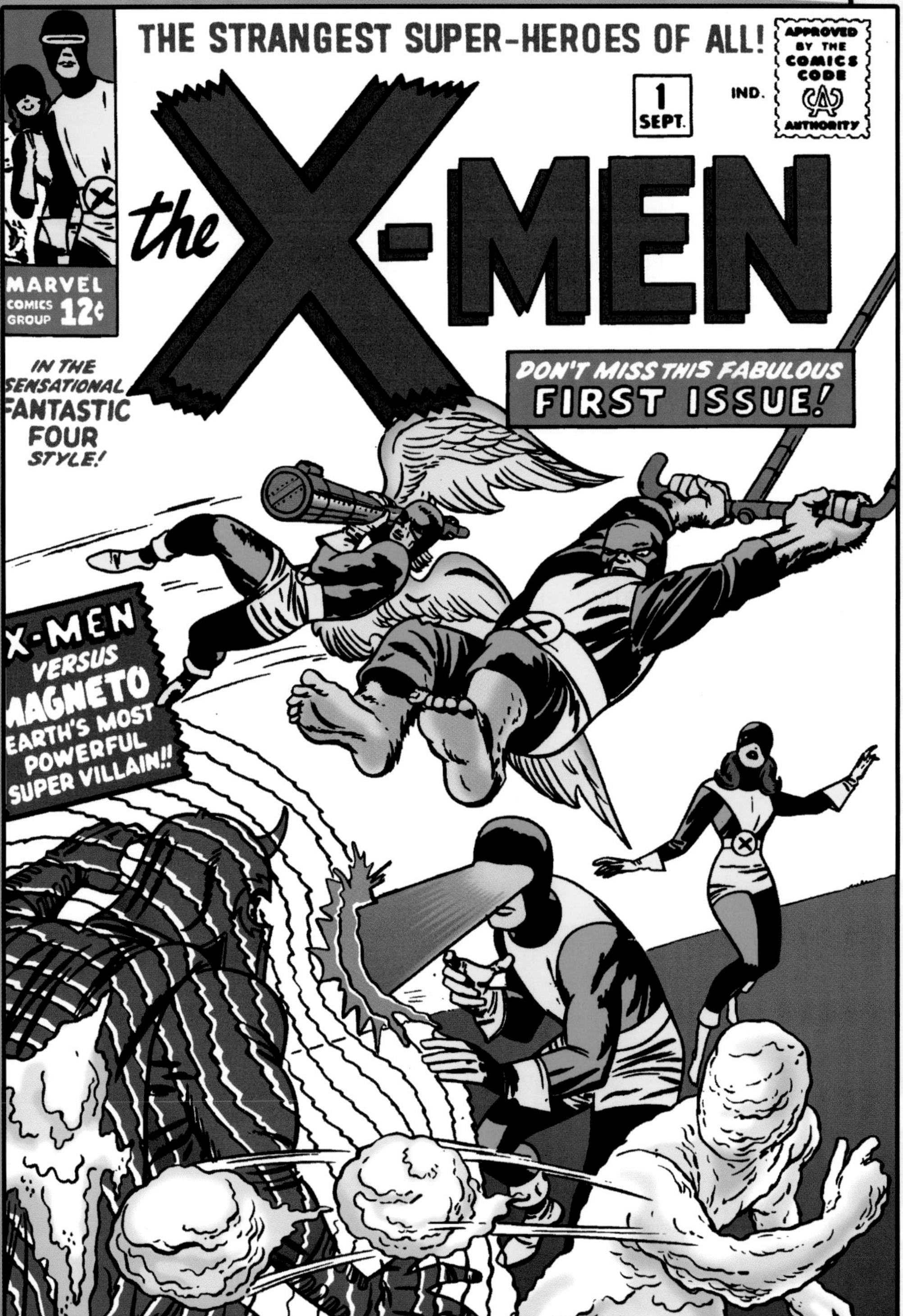
THE STRANGEST SUPER-HEROES OF ALL!
APPROVED BY THE COMICS CODE AUTHORITY
1 SEPT.
IND.
the X-MEN
MARVEL COMICS GROUP 12¢
IN THE SENSATIONAL FANTASTIC FOUR STYLE!
DON'T MISS THIS FABULOUS FIRST ISSUE!
X-MEN VERSUS MAGNETO EARTH'S MOST POWERFUL SUPER VILLAIN!!

THE REAL WORLD

While Lee and Kirby were adding to superhero mythology, major events were taking place in the world around them. One of these was the civil rights movement. Although the law had long stated that all Americans were to be treated equally, they often were not. Many African Americans and other minorities, aided by people of all backgrounds, were organizing to gain equal rights. Perhaps, in some way, the idea of a persecuted minority seeking to be treated like everyone else was an inspiration for the creation of the X-Men. As prominent X-Men comic writer Chris Claremont says about the comic series in Gerard Jones and Will Jacobs's *The Comic Book Heroes*, "What we have here, intended or not, is a book about racism, bigotry, and prejudice."

That the X-Men were teenagers was also important. In childhood, everything is taken care of for you, but your choices are restricted.

WHAT'S AN "X-MAN"?

When Marvel writer and editor in chief Stan Lee proposed the series that would become *The X-Men* to his boss, publisher Martin Goodman, it was called *The Mutants*.

Goodman liked the idea but not the name. He thought no one—especially not a child—would know what a "mutant" was. So Lee came up with the name X-Men, for the extra power that each member of the team had.

While that wouldn't be clear until a reader had actually read the first issue, and it could be argued that no one would know what an X-Man was anymore than they'd know what a mutant was, Goodman liked it, and the rest is history.

The X-Men first appeared during a time of change in the United States. Here, Dr. Martin Luther King, Jr. and his wife, Coretta Scott King, lead a voting rights march in Alabama on March 30, 1965. The conflicts of the times were echoed in the X-Men stories about prejudice, with some readers seeing hatred of mutants being used as a metaphor for hating people because of their race or religion.

As an adult, you have more freedom but also more responsibility. In *The X-Men*, children could see a fantastic version of what being a teen might be like. Teenagers saw stories of teens who, despite having superpowers, were picked on by the world. And the X-Men still had to answer to their teacher, Professor X, even when they disagreed with him. Any kid or teen could relate to that. Best of all, they weren't called the "X-Kids" or the "X-Teens." They were the X-Men. In the popular culture of the 1950s and 1960s, teens struggling to be taken seriously were important figures. From the drama of movies like *Rebel Without a Cause* to the comedy of "beach party" movies, teens were eager to see stories about their struggles growing up.

SUPER HERO HIGH SCHOOL

The idea of kids in a school setting was something of a risk. While comics of the time portrayed parents and teachers as positive figures, it was assumed that no kid wanted to read a story about school. They were in school all day, the reasoning went, so they wouldn't want it in their entertainment. And teachers were the "enemies" who made them do things they didn't want to.

But the X-Men liked and respected Professor X, and he them. Why did young readers accept this? For one thing, Xavier wasn't that much older than they were. While he aged a bit over the years, he seemed at first to be no more than ten years older than his students. Secondly, Xavier was, like them, a mutant and able to understand them in a way that "normal" kids could not. He was also able to relate to them in ways their families and teachers in other schools could not.

The X-Men showed that a school setting doesn't have to be a metaphor for keeping kids down as knowledge is force-fed into their brains. At the Xavier school, the students majored in becoming Super Heroes! That's a pretty cool way to spend the school day. Also, there never seemed to be any math or English classes going on at Xavier's school— just Super Hero training in the Danger Room. There were even battles with Super Villains—such as Xavier's evil stepbrother, the Juggernaut—that took place at the school.

For a child or teenager, school is where much of the drama of their lives happens. Making friends, learning new things, dealing with bullies, and learning about romance often happen in school. Although *The X-Men* started out as a series about a school for young mutants, it was destined to grow from that into much more.

In this page from *The X-Men* #13, the unstoppable Juggernaut invades the Xavier School. The message was clear: being a student at Xavier wasn't about a boring day of classes. Students of the school had to use their mutant powers to save mankind on a regular basis. The script is by Stan Lee, with art by Jack Kirby, Werner Roth (using the name Jay Gavin), and Joe Sinnott.

3 FROM CULT TO SUPERSTARDOM

Anyone who has ever felt picked on because of his size, the color of his hair, or the fact that he likes to read comic books can relate to the X-Men, who are hated because they are different. Anyone who has ever been excluded from a club at school and then sought friendship with others who were also excluded can relate to the X-Men as well. Being excluded sometimes leads to—or comes from—the victim feeling he or she is somehow better than those who keep him or her out. Because the X-Men are superior, at least in terms of their abilities, they appeal to anyone who has ever felt left out. That means everybody. This is one of the prime fantasies the idea of the superhero appeals to: "If only people knew my real power! Then they would love me—or even fear me."

This popular theme of persecution would echo throughout *The X-Men*, but despite that, the series didn't really catch on in a big way at the beginning. The series was fairly successful, but Lee and Kirby didn't stay with it long. Other writers and artists came and went, but no one put their personal stamp on the series. The last new story of the first X-Men series appeared in issue #66 in 1970. Only reprints of previous issues continued to be published.

ALL NEW, ALL DIFFERENT!

In 1975, a large market for translated American comics had developed all over the world. It was suggested to Marvel's then editor in chief, Roy Thomas, that a team made up of heroes from a variety of countries would be popular in those countries. Thomas and writer Len Wein decided to remake *The X-Men* into an international team.

Wein and artist Dave Cockrum came up with the new X-Men team. Cockrum had had a very popular run on DC's *Legion of Super Heroes*. He had many ideas for new and exciting characters. Chris Claremont, then an assistant editor at Marvel, also contributed ideas to the new version of the series.

Wein and Cockrum took Professor X and Cyclops from the old team and surrounded them with a new team made up of mutants from many countries. These included Wolverine from Canada, Colossus from the USSR, and Banshee from Ireland.

By the time the new team debuted in *Giant-Size X-Men* #1 in 1975, the original desire to specifically target foreign audiences was forgotten. But it had given the team a unique, international flavor,

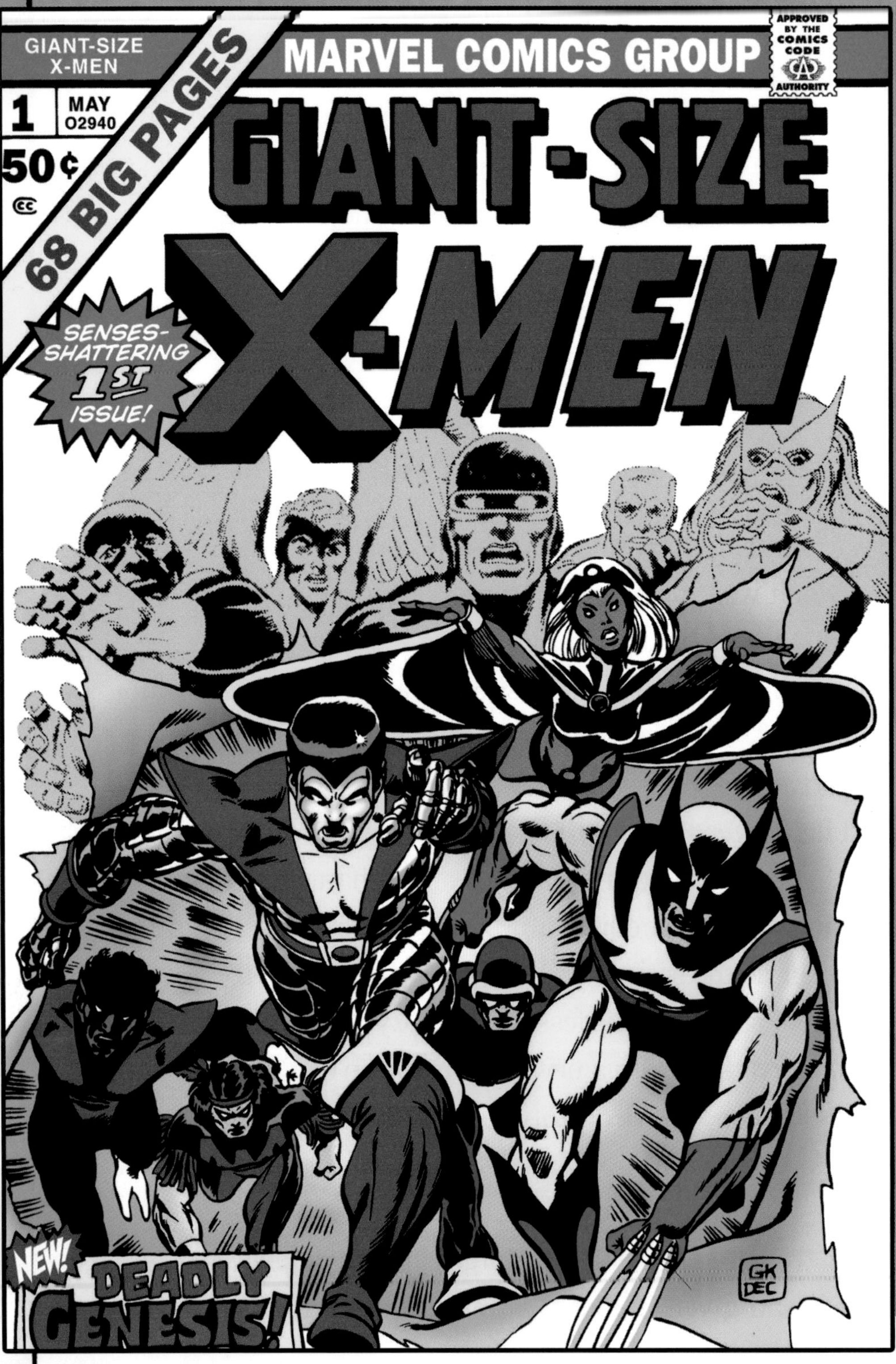
GIANT-SIZE
X-MEN
68 BIG PAGES
MARVEL COMICS GROUP
APPROVED BY THE COMICS CODE AUTHORITY
1
MAY
02940
50¢
GIANT-SIZE
X-MEN
SENSES-SHATTERING 1ST ISSUE!
NEW!
DEADLY GENESIS!
GK DEC

with members from many countries, even ones that had no translation deals with Marvel.

The new team's second adventure appeared in *The X-Men* #94. (Marvel had been reprinting old X-Men adventures since the last new story appeared in issue #66.) Claremont was credited as cowriter on the issue. By issue #97, he was writing the title on his own. Claremont would go on to write *The X-Men* (and many related series and one-shot comics) for the next fifteen years. He returned to *The X-Men* in 2000 and continues to write adventures of the X-Men today.

Under Wein (as writer and editor), Claremont, and Cockrum, as well as editors Marv Wolfman and Thomas, *The X-Men* became a hit. Perhaps people had caught up with the concept of a persecuted group of heroes trying to do the right thing for a world that hated them.

The co-creators always made sure to use, but not to be confined by, the prejudice angle. The X-Men became involved in all kinds of adventures. They traveled to outer space and to a hidden jungle called the Savage Land. While battling aliens and dinosaurs, they still fought mutants and mutant-haters and everything else Claremont and Cockrum could throw at them.

In 1974, the X-Men comic was relaunched in *Giant-Size X-Men* #1. Seen here is the cover, by Gil Kane and Dave Cockrum. This comic book was an experiment to see if a new version of the team, featuring mutants from many countries, would be more popular than the original series. The experiment was a huge success. The X-Men became a tremendous hit on TV and in the movies as well as in comics.

MR. X-MEN

In college, Claremont had studied to be an actor. He brought a theatrical flair to the stories he wrote. Like Stan Lee, he realized that the best stories weren't about just the action and adventure, but about the drama of people blessed—and cursed—with superhuman powers. As Claremont says in Michael Mallory's *Marvel: The Characters and Their Universe*, the X-Men were "a group of characters that [readers] embraced, rooted for, and wanted to see what happened next in their lives."

When Cockrum left as artist to be replaced by John Byrne, the revived series kept its initial energy and built upon it. As the stories grew in scope, they deepened in character development. A memorable peak was the famous "Dark Phoenix Saga," in which Jean Grey (Marvel Girl) gained enormous power and called herself the Phoenix. This was because she had seemingly returned to life after being killed on a mission, as the phoenix of legend had returned to life. When her power was at full force, she gave off flaming energy that took the shape of a hawklike bird.

When Jean's mind was twisted by the X-Men's old enemy Mastermind, the Phoenix became a force for destruction. She even

It doesn't get any more classic than this scene from 1978's *X-Men* #112 (script by Chris Claremont, art by John Byrne and Terry Austin). In it, the X-Men's longtime enemy, Magneto, battles Cyclops and Phoenix (formerly known as Jean Grey or Marvel Girl). In the X-Men movies, Magneto is played by Ian McKellen, Cyclops by James Marsden, and Jean by Famke Janssen.

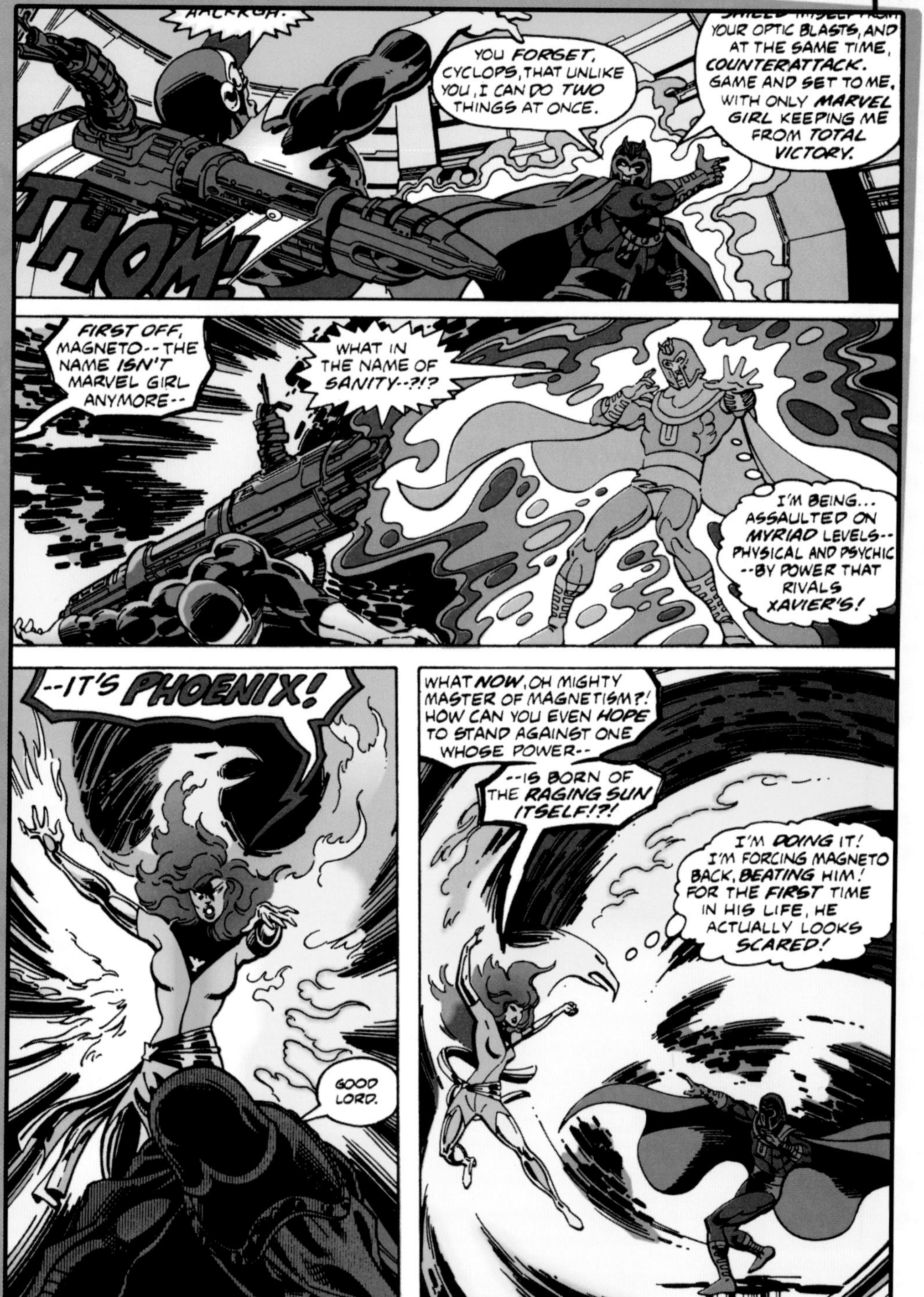
YOU FORGET, CYCLOPS, THAT UNLIKE YOU, I CAN DO TWO THINGS AT ONCE.
YOUR OPTIC BLASTS, AND AT THE SAME TIME, COUNTERATTACK. GAME AND SET TO ME, WITH ONLY MARVEL GIRL KEEPING ME FROM TOTAL VICTORY.
THOM!
FIRST OFF, MAGNETO--THE NAME ISN'T MARVEL GIRL ANYMORE--
WHAT IN THE NAME OF SANITY--?!?
I'M BEING... ASSAULTED ON MYRIAD LEVELS--PHYSICAL AND PSYCHIC--BY POWER THAT RIVALS XAVIER'S!
--IT'S PHOENIX!
GOOD LORD.
WHAT NOW, OH MIGHTY MASTER OF MAGNETISM?! HOW CAN YOU EVEN HOPE TO STAND AGAINST ONE WHOSE POWER--
--IS BORN OF THE RAGING SUN ITSELF!?!
I'M DOING IT! I'M FORCING MAGNETO BACK, BEATING HIM! FOR THE FIRST TIME IN HIS LIFE, HE ACTUALLY LOOKS SCARED!
HER POWER IS A SONG WITHIN HER, FILLING HER WITH A PRIMAL GLORY, AN UNHUMAN JOY THAT SHE'S BEGINNING TO ENJOY MORE AND MORE.

destroyed an entire planet! In a controversial storyline, she was put on trial for her crimes and died for them.

Killing such a popular character was unheard of in comics. The ending was ordered by then editor in chief Jim Shooter. He believed that a Marvel hero who killed had to be punished. His involvement was seen as unfair meddling by some within the comic industry.

Still, the result of this storyline was that the series became more popular than ever. Editors, including Louise Jones and Ann Nocenti, and artists, including Paul Smith, John Romita Jr., and the returning Cockrum himself, came and went. However, Claremont remained on board as the writer of every issue of *The X-Men* until 1991.

"DAYS OF FUTURE PAST"

In 1981, *The X-Men* #141 and #142 came out. "Days of Future Past," as the two-part story was titled, painted a bleak future where giant mutant-hunting robots called Sentinels ruled over an enslaved world.

In addition to being a powerful story that showed an older Wolverine, as well as the tragic fates of many of his teammates, it was the first in what would become an almost sub-universe of X-Men stories showing possible futures.

Alternate-future stories showing what would become of the X-Men, and of the entire human race, have been featured in such storylines as "Age of Apocalypse." Fans can't seem to get enough of stories about possible fates of the characters.

POPULARITY SOARS!

Through the 1980s and 1990s, *The X-Men* spawned literally dozens of series, miniseries, and graphic novels. These all featured groupings or solo adventures of various old and new X-Men and supporting characters. The first was *The New Mutants*, a series about Professor X organizing a new team of teenage mutants. At one point in the early 1990s, there were more than twenty different comic books featuring characters from *The X-Men* published in any given month.

Why, after so many years and so many types of Super Heroes, did the X-Men become so much more popular than any others?

4 NOT YOUR FATHER'S SUPER HEROES

The X-Men concept embodies many metaphors, while also providing cool characters and exciting stories. One key X-Men metaphor is the idea of family. As Gerard Jones and Will Jacobs say in their book *The Comic Book Heroes*, "The X-Men were a family, and like a family they kept growing and had to keep negotiating their relationships." The X-Men are misunderstood, feared, and hated by the world. This often includes the families from which they came. To many children and teenagers since the early 1960s and beyond in the United States, this would have been a metaphor for the sense of unease set into play by the growing divorce rate in the country. For them, the family couldn't be depended upon in the same ways it had been. Through the X-Men, they could imagine what it would be like to create and exist in a family of people just like themselves. It's unlikely that Lee and Kirby intentionally tried to express such feelings in *The X-Men*. But they were living in a culture where such things were part of everyday life. It was bound to seep into the stories they produced.

Lee and Kirby especially could not have been immune, as mentioned earlier, to the changes being brought about by the civil rights movement. While *The X-Men* started as another way to portray Super Heroes, it slowly became a metaphor for the evils of prejudice of any kind. But it wasn't until the series was relaunched in the 1970s that a clear message was seen in *The X-Men* by both its creators and its audience. The country was reeling from controversy over the Vietnam War. People strongly disagreed on the United States' involvement in this conflict.

The values of the entire society were starting to change at the time the X-Men and the other Marvel characters were created. Those changes continued into the 1970s. What Lee and Kirby had started, Claremont and Cockrum, and then Claremont and Byrne, were able to take to levels beyond what anyone thought could be done in a Super Hero comic book.

A NEW GENERATION

As young people themselves, the writer and artists of the *All-New, All-Different X-Men* (as the relaunched series was for a time called) had grown up in a changing world. Also, many of the new creators came from the ranks of comic fandom. As children and teenagers, they read *The Fantastic Four*, *Spider-Man*, and the other Marvel titles. They knew

The co-creator most associated with the X-Men, from the 1970s to the present, is Chris Claremont. He started as an assistant contributing ideas to the team's 1974 relaunch. Claremont was soon the writer of *The X-Men* and many of its spin-off titles, such as *The New Mutants* and *Wolverine*.

what had come before and, as fans, had a sense for what their new audience wanted. This audience wasn't just children. It was increasingly made up of college students and young adults.

Today, many fans admire writers and illustrators as much as the characters whose stories they tell. Comic creators have become celebrities. Claremont made himself the public face of *The X-Men*. He attended countless comic conventions. At these "cons," he got to meet many of *The X-Men*'s fans. Claremont made comic creators realize the deep bond their audiences have with them. He showed how this could create dedicated fans, creators who know what their audience wants, and higher sales for the publisher.

Claremont, Cockrum, and Byrne co-created a very dense fictional universe for their characters. By its nature, a team story is complicated. There are five or more heroes and many villains to keep track of. The subplots can become very messy. Every character has a family, a love interest, and a personality that make him or her different from other characters. Instead of trying to simplify the characters and stories, the creators gambled that readers would enjoy such complexity.

They were proven right. The web of plots and subplots that made up *The X-Men* line of comics appealed to readers. The skill of the creators was high enough that the plot threads always progressed in each issue. However, over the years some plotlines have been left dangling. Some mysteries have been drawn out longer than creators and readers would have wanted.

WOLVERINE

The most famous of these long-term mysteries would have to be that of Wolverine's origin. For years, how the man called Logan came to be Wolverine was only hinted at. Bits and pieces of his past were revealed, but the full story of who he really was, even of how old he was, had never been told.

WOLVERINE'S BREAKOUT SUCCESS

Wolverine first appeared in 1974's *The Incredible Hulk* #180 and #181, which came out before the new *X-Men* was relaunched. Roy Thomas, the editor in chief at the time, came up with the name and that Wolverine would be "a little, scrappy guy." Len Wein wrote the story, and artist John Romita Sr. designed the character, which may have been inspired by an early Dave Cockrum sketch.

The co-creators liked the character so much they decided to put him in the new, internationally flavored X-Men team. He quickly became the most popular team member. When the first X-Men movie was cast, comic fans were concerned that the six-foot-three-inch-tall Hugh Jackman was too tall to play the five-foot–three-inch-tall mutant. But when the film came out, they realized that Jackman captured the spirit of the Canadian X-Man completely.

Wolverine cuts loose against a flying dinosaur in the danger-filled Savage Land. Energetic artwork (like John Byrne and Terry Austin's shown here) is a big part of why readers the world over responded so strongly to the clawed mutant. This page is from *The X-Men* #114. The script, of course, is by Chris Claremont.

Wolverine himself has proven to be the most popular hero to come from *The X-Men*. His appeal is similar to that of the Thing in *The Fantastic Four*. Wolverine is a scrappy, hotheaded guy who's always ready for a fight. He makes wisecracks even under pressure. Plus, he's got those cool claws that shoot out of the backs of his hands!

More than that, he is a man of honor, living by a strict code that's constantly at war with his animal-like nature. He was the first X-Man to have his own series, which continues to this day. There's even talk of a Wolverine movie spinning off from the X-Men films.

At last, in 2001, the *Wolverine: Origin* limited series came out. It spilled the beans about many of his secrets, including his age and how he first came to be called Wolverine. Some fans loved it, and some hated it. But they all bought it because everyone was curious to see just what Wolverine's true story was.

5 IT'S AN X-MEN WORLD

Marvel Comics in general, and the X-Men in particular, changed forever how people see Super Heroes. *The X-Men* comics are the next step in Super Hero development.

In comics, the effects of the X-Men's popularity were clearly evident. Every company had to have a super-team of young people from different backgrounds who fought strange menaces and didn't get along with each other.

Marvel itself put out many comics that spun off of *The X-Men* comics. Besides *The New Mutants*, there were *X-Force*, *Excalibur*, and *Generation X*. Marvel series *The New Warriors* and *Runaways* are about mostly nonmutant Super Heroes. However, any Super Hero series that comes out, from any company, will always be compared to *The X-Men*. It set the standard and not just in comic books.

THEY CHANGED EVERYTHING

In other media, the X-Men's effect was equally powerful.

Do you like *Buffy the Vampire Slayer*? How about Harry Potter? If so, then you've got *The X-Men* to thank. *The X-Men*, even more than *The Fantastic Four*, took the hero-group idea and stood it on its head. The X-Men version of the Marvel approach has been influential throughout popular culture. Today, a story about a team of heroes that doesn't argue and trip themselves up is the exception.

Creators of action-adventure movies and TV shows strive to produce blockbusters that will appeal to people of all ages, genders, and cultures. As often as not, creators use X-Men-flavored stories to achieve this goal. Even in non-Super Hero stories, the mix of action and soap-opera elements used is largely due to the influence of *The X-Men*.

By the 1970s, action-adventure stories were being created for movies and television that appealed to both adults and children. *Star Wars* is the most famous example of such material. Many of the creators of such stories were readers and fans of Marvel comics,

DARK WILLOW

In the 2002 *Buffy the Vampire Slayer* TV series episode "Two to Go," Buffy's friend Willow's magic powers go wildly out of control. At one point, another character says she's "like Dark Phoenix."

Buffy creator Joss Whedon has said that Buffy herself was inspired by X-Men team member Kitty Pryde (aka Shadowcat). So it's not a surprise that he would refer to a favorite X-Men character and storyline in a *Buffy* episode. Whedon has gone on to become a writer of acclaimed X-Men comic books.

Buffy the Vampire Slayer creator Joss Whedon was a huge fan of The X-men. He finally got the chance to put his mark on the characters that he so enjoyed with Marvel's *Astonishing X-Men* series. Whedon, along with artist John Cassaday, brought the sharp dialogue and quirky humor of *Buffy* to the X-Men universe that had inspired him. The panel from *Astonishing* #12 shows Wolverine, Kitty Pryde, Colossus, and Emma Frost battling robots.

including *The X-Men*. They learned from Marvel that a story could be told so as to appeal to different readers in different ways. A younger reader might be most interested in the action. A teen might be more involved with the characters' emotions. An adult might enjoy seeing references to current events or stories that deal with more serious ideas, even if those ideas came packaged in a story of super-human battles.

Marvel decided to try to bring in new readers by starting a new series called *Ultimate X-Men*. *Ultimate* reinvented the X-Men, bringing in a feel similar to that featured in the movies. This Stuart Immonen illustration is from *Ultimate X-Men* #65.

Buffy and her team of helpers were certainly inspired by *The X-Men*. Harry Potter's school setting, where gifted youngsters are trained in using their special abilities, is another version of the X-Men's situation. In fact, many fictional school or work situations where people with special abilities who don't know each other are forced to work together may have been inspired by *The X-Men*.

NEW FRONTIERS

It was only a matter of time before the X-Men themselves appeared in other media. *The X-Men* animated series, which debuted in 1992, proved that kids would watch a show that had emotional depth along with colorful characters and exciting action. It also proved that children would watch "to be continued" cartoon stories. Until then, it was rare for any cartoon story to go beyond a single episode.

The *X-Men* movies have shown that audiences around the world and of all ages can relate to the different elements that make the

X-Men unique. Interestingly, many of the children who watched the animated series grew up to be fans of the movies. Many of them may never have even read an *X-Men* comic book. Moreover, the X-Men also star in popular video games.

The X-Men have become as well known as Tarzan, Sherlock Holmes, and James Bond. Their influence on our action-adventure entertainment, whether in comic books, on television, in the movies, or in games, is lasting and permanent. The X-Men were a product of their times, but they have helped shape the popular culture of several generations.

TIMELINE: THE X-MEN'S CREATORS

1917 Jack Kirby is born on August 28 in New York City.

1922 Stan Lee is born on December 28 in New York City.

1940 Lee goes to work at Martin Goodman's Timely Comics. Roy Thomas is born in Missouri. Kirby joins Timely as staff artist.

1950 Chris Claremont is born in London, England.

1961 Lee and Kirby co-create *The Fantastic Four* and launch what has come to be known as the Marvel Age of Comics. Atlas is now called Marvel Comics.

1963 Lee and Kirby co-create *The Avengers* and *The X-Men*.

1969 Bard College student Claremont gets a summer internship at Marvel.

1974 Claremont becomes an assistant editor at Marvel and writer of *Iron Fist*, a series drawn by John Byrne.

1975 Writer Len Wein and artist Dave Cockrum relaunch the X-Men in *Giant-Size X-Men* #1. Claremont begins as a writer of *The X-Men* with #94.

1979 John Byrne becomes an artist for *The X-Men*.

1991 Claremont leaves *The X-Men* and Marvel.

1992 *The X-Men* animated series premieres on the Fox network.

1994 Jack Kirby dies.

2000 *X-Men* the movie, directed by Bryan Singer, premieres. Claremont returns to the X-Men comics.

1963   *The X-Men* #1 introduces the X-Men and their greatest foe, Magneto.

1964   *The X-Men* #4 introduces the Brotherhood of Evil Mutants.

1970   The last new X-Men story until 1975 is published.

1975   The X-Men are relaunched in *Giant-Size X-Men* #1 and *The X-Men* #94.

1980   Jean Grey becomes Dark Phoenix in *The X-Men* #134.
Jean Grey apparently dies in *The X-Men* #137.

1981   *The X-Men* #141 and #142: "Days of Future Past."

1982   The first X-Men spin-off series, *The New Mutants*, debuts.
The *Wolverine* limited series begins.

1985   Jean Grey returns in *The Fantastic Four* #286.

1988   The *Wolverine* ongoing series begins.

1994   Cyclops and Jean Grey marry in *The X-Men* (second series) #30.

2001   The *Wolverine: Origin* limited series begins.

GLOSSARY

comic convention A gathering of comic book fans and professionals to meet each other, discuss comics and related topics, and buy and sell old and new comic books and related items. The largest convention in the United States is Comic-Con International, held each summer in San Diego, California.

editor The person who oversees the work of writers, artists, and others who work on comic books. The editor represents the publisher to the creative staff and the creative staff to the publisher.

fandom The overall name given to devoted fans of comic books or of a specific comic book series or character.

genre A type of story defined by a set of traits. Superhero genre stories involve heroes and villains with amazing powers.

graphic novel A long comic book that may be a new story or a collection of previously printed stories.

juggernaut A massive object, movement, campaign, or force that crushes everything in its path.

metaphor Something used to represent another thing or an idea, in order to explain the thing or idea more clearly or in a way that is more acceptable.

miniseries A comic book story that is told in a set number of issues. It has an intended ending and a preplanned number of issues. Miniseries are sometimes collected into graphic novels. Also called limited series.

mutation A significant change in a member of a species.

origin Beginning. In superhero comic books, the origin is usually the story in which a character gets powers and a costume.

prejudice A feeling or opinion about someone or something formed without firsthand knowledge about the person or thing.

publisher The person or company that is responsible for arranging the business-related issues of creating and selling printed material.

sidekick The assistant and companion to a superhero. Usually a child or teenager.

subplot A second story in a work of fiction that happens at the same time as the main story. It is usually of lesser importance.

superhero A being with amazing powers who often disguises his or her true identity and wears a colorful costume.

The International Comic Arts Association
533 Johnson Avenue
Morris, IL 60450
(815) 942-1819
Web site: http://www.comicarts.org/index.php

Museum of Comic and Cartoon Art
594 Broadway, Suite 401
New York, NY 10012
(212) 254-3511
Web site: http://www.moccany.org

WEB SITES

Due to the changing nature of Internet links, the Rosen Publishing Group, Inc., has developed an online list of Web sites related to the subject of this book. This site is updated regularly. Please use this link to access the list:

http://www.rosenlinks.com/crah/xmen

You can also refer to the Marvel Web site:

http://www.marvel.com

FOR FURTHER READING

Claremont, Chris, Dave Cockrum, John Byrne, et al. *Essential X-Men*, Vol. 1. New York, NY: Marvel Comics, 1996.

Claremont, Chris, Frank Miller, and Josef Rubinstein. *Wolverine*. New York, NY: Marvel Comics, 1990.

Jemas, Bill, Mark Millar, and Paul Jenkins. *Wolverine: Origin*. New York, NY: Marvel Comics, 2002.

Kirby, Jack, Stan Lee, and Joe Simon. *Marvel Visionaries: Jack Kirby*. New York, NY: Marvel Comics, 2004.

Lee, Stan, and Jack Kirby. *Marvel Masterworks: The X-Men*. New York, NY: Marvel Enterprises, 1998.

Lee, Stan, Jack Kirby, Steve Ditko, and John Romita. *Marvel Visionaries: Stan Lee*. New York, NY: Marvel Comics, 2005.

Simon, Joe, and Jack Kirby. *Marvel Masterworks: Golden Age Captain America*, Vol. 1. New York, NY: Marvel Comics, 2005.

BIBLIOGRAPHY

Daniels, Les. *Marvel: Five Fabulous Decades of the World's Greatest Comics.* New York, NY: Harry N. Abrams, 1991.

Feiffer, Jules. *The Great Comic Book Heroes.* New York, NY: Dial Press, 1965.

Jones, Gerard, and Will Jacobs. *The Comic Book Heroes.* Rocklin, CA: Prima Publishing, 1997.

Kirby, Jack, with Mark Evanier and Steve Sherman. *Kirby Unleashed.* Raleigh, NC: TwoMorrows, 2004.

Lee, Stan. *Son of Origins of Marvel Comics.* Rev. ed. New York, NY: Marvel Comics, 1997.

Lee, Stan, and George Mair. *Excelsior! The Amazing Life of Stan Lee.* New York, NY: Fireside, 2002.

Mallory, Michael. *Marvel: The Characters and Their Universe.* New York, NY: Hugh Lauter Levin Associates, 2001.

Sanderson, Peter. *Marvel Universe.* New York, NY: Harry N. Abrams, 1996.

Simon, Joe. *The Comic Book Makers.* New York, NY: Crestwood/II Publications, 1990.

Steranko, James. *The Steranko History of Comics*, Vol.1. Reading, PA: Supergraphics, 1970.

Yesterdayland. "Stan Lee Interview." Retrieved February 21, 2002 (http://web.archive.org/web/20010609215240/www.yesterdayland.com/features/interviews/lee_s.php).

INDEX

ABOUT THE AUTHOR

Danny Fingeroth was a writer and editor at Marvel Comics for many years. He worked on many famous characters, including Spider-Man and the X-Men. He is the author of *Superman on the Couch: What Superheroes Really Tell Us About Ourselves and Our Society* (Continuum, 2004) and produces *Write Now!*, a magazine about writing for comics and animation, published by TwoMorrows.

PHOTO CREDITS

p. 10 © Frank Trapper/Corbis; p. 12 courtesy of the Kirby Estate and the Jack Kirby Collector magazine (www.twomorrows.com) © Kirby Estate; p. 19 © Getty Images, Inc.; p. 32 © Jonah Weiland/ CBR. All other images provided by Marvel Entertainment, Inc.

Designer: Thomas Forget
Editor: Leigh Ann Cobb
Photo Researcher: Les Kanturek